Praise for *It's OK to Say "They"*

This book is a must-read for anyone who works with children! We all face the topic of transgender and nonbinary students, with different levels of experience. As teachers, we are here to educate and make our students feel loved, safe, and accepted. We must continue to do what is best for ALL students. The world is evolving in new and different directions, and so must our teaching! This book shows the importance of educators making the slightest changes in order to become allies to transgender and nonbinary students. These changes in how we address and accept all students can have lasting effects.—Kristine Jussaume, fourth-grade teacher, Norman E. Day School

It's OK to Say "They" illustrates the impact we, as teachers, have in our expressions of acceptance, validation, and openness on our students and the society they are growing in. This sets the foundation for all other learning. The powerful insights and practices provided by this book remind us of our tremendous responsibility to turn anxiety into hope, insecurity into determination, and isolation into welcome.—Bernie Bluhm, MEd, New England College

Thank you, Dr. Whittlesey, for giving me a practical approach to creating a learning environment where students of all backgrounds feel safe, included, and welcomed! The personal accounts of those interviewed paired with your straightforward strategies have allowed me to promote an inclusive educational atmosphere where all can thrive socially, emotionally, and intellectually.—Leah M. Ferullo, EdD, Winchester Public Schools

As a parent of two nonbinary children who both use they/them/their pronouns and the coordinator of social emotional learning for a public school system, I enthusiastically recommend this thoughtful and helpful book! It is an invaluable resource for educators and parents. The more we understand youth who identify as transgender and nonbinary, the better we can support their academic, social, and emotional success. There are alarming rates of suicide and suicide attempts for transgender youth, and current research shows how critical the support of just *one* adult can be. This book prepares our educators to be those adults, especially for children who don't have support systems outside of school.

—Larainne M. Wilson, MEd, coordinator of social emotional learning and counseling, Chelmsford High School

Finally! All educators want to provide support to transgender and nonbinary students, but most are not really sure how to do so. This groundbreaking book provides detailed strategies and language to support all students. Hearing directly from students within the book not only makes it more powerful but will open your eyes as to what they go through on a daily basis. *It's OK to Say "They"* will work great as the subject for a professional study group or as the basis for much-needed professional development.

—Matthew L. Beyranevand, EdD, math teacher and author of *Teach Math Like This, Not Like That* and *Adding Parents to the Equation*

As a nonbinary person who often had to make the difficult choice between expressing my own gender identity or protecting my personal safety in school, I am beyond grateful that this trailblazing book exists as a resource for educators and ultimately the well-being of our youth. Compassionate and supportive teachers can create relationships with LGBTQ youth that have lasting impacts. This book equips our educators with knowledge and understanding that can quite literally save lives.—Fernando Z. López, executive director, San Diego LGBT Pride

It's OK to Say "They" is a must-read for educators everywhere. Whittlesey seamlessly interweaves practical, accessible tips for allies with educational (and sometimes heartbreaking) first-person accounts from students. By enacting this book's suggestions for improving trans inclusivity in the classroom and beyond, educators have the opportunity to change and even save students' lives. —Molly Woodstock, gender educator and host of the Gender Reveal podcast.

It's OK to Say "They" is an essential read for educators looking to be an ally for ALL students. This is one of the most powerful and practical resources for educators on creating an inclusive classroom and school environment. The tips of practice are spot-on, and the accounts from student experiences formidable. This book comes at a time when our schools need to improve our practices to ensure the safety and well-being of all students. Praise for Dr. Whittlesey as a fierce advocate on this topic.—Dr. Molly McMahon, principal, South Row Elementary School

This book is a superb resource for educators, parents, and other allies of transgender students, providing needed clarification on "dead names," pronouns, classroom policies, and other important challenges classroom teachers face working with non-cisgendered students in today's schools. This handbook rings true with authentic advice. Grounded in the research of an award-winning dissertation, *It's OK to Say "They"* shares the words of transgender students and the teachers and administrators who work with them. The handbook offers action-oriented suggestions for making school better for everyone. An experienced teacher and administrator herself, Dr. Whittlesey knows what works and why we should do it.—Judith Davidson, PhD, College of Education, University of Massachusetts Lowell College

It's OK to Say "They"

Tips for Educator Allies of Transgender and Nonbinary Students

Christy Whittlesey, PhD

Illustrations by Mordecai Vezina

This book is available at special discounts when purchased in quantity for use as premiums, promotions, fundraisers, or educational purposes. For inquiries and details, contact the publisher at books@daveburgessconsulting.com.

Published by Dave Burgess Consulting, Inc.
San Diego, CA
DaveBurgessConsulting.com

Library of Congress Control Number: 2019950054
Paperback ISBN: 978-1-949595-89-5
Ebook ISBN: 978-1-949595-90-1

Cover design by Kachergis Book Design
Interior design by Kachergis Book Design

It's OK to Say "They"

" In middle school and high school, I was always dealing with a bit of sadness looming … I would have trouble remembering my homework: to write it down, to do it. Sometimes I couldn't focus so it would take me hours to do it, so in general the academic part of high school was not something that I enjoyed at all. "

The Problem

We all know that students can't learn when they don't feel safe. When they are victimized, bullied, or discounted, their ability to engage in classroom learning is impeded, and their self-esteem nosedives. This dynamic presents acute challenges for transgender and nonbinary students, who are forced to navigate the rigid gender-binary system in place in schools. After all, schools were built to accommodate two genders: boys and girls. This gender-binary system extends from buildings and facilities (restrooms, locker rooms), to class structures (boys/girls PE classes or choral classes), to curriculum, and beyond—including teachers' classroom practices.

The problem with the gender-binary system is that it does not acknowledge or accommodate those who do not identify with their assigned gender at birth, those who identify with multiple genders, or those who do not identify with a gender at all.

Within the gender-binary system of schools, some educators are simply not aware of the issues that transgender or nonbinary students face. Others want to support these youths but are afraid of doing the "wrong" thing—so they do nothing.

In the worst cases, educators may act upon personal bias or transphobia. Harassment of LGBTQ students by teachers is a well-documented problem in research literature.

"High school was the first time I realized that grown-ups can be bullies too. I had to take a class for two weeks in the secretary's office because I was so afraid of my class. They would throw down my backpack and throw paper at me and call me Caitlyn Jenner, and my teacher would laugh, and then when I would say something, he'd say, "Well, that's just guys messing around, and you're one of the guys now, right?""

" I was terrified of everybody around me because of how bad the bullying got and how bad getting beaten up got. I was distracted by a lot of things. My academics didn't really take priority because of my mental health. "

The result? Students who do not fall into neat gender categories often experience intense struggles with school that can manifest socially, emotionally, and academically. In fact, transgender and nonbinary students experience significantly lower levels of academic success than their cisgender peers, while at the same time suffering from significantly increased rates of anxiety, depression, and suicide.

This may not come as a surprise: after all, these students are already dealing with the school and social stressors that accompany kids from childhood to adolescence to young adulthood. On top of that, they are regularly reminded that they do not "fit" into where they spend the majority of each day for ten months out of the year. These reminders can be subtle or violent—but they are pervasive.

In addition, other identifiers such as race, class, ability, religion, and nationality can put students at higher risk for being targeted. For example, an inordinately high number of transgender youths of color are murdered each year.

In light of transgender and nonbinary students' negative experiences in schools, it's clear that supportive, inclusive approaches and policies that are enforced by all members of a school community are necessary for these students to experience success as they develop emotionally, socially, and academically.

Addressing the Problem

If you want to make an impact, but you're not sure where to start, good news. By reading this book, you're making a conscious effort to become an educator ally to our transgender and nonbinary students—and school environments where adults are supportive and understanding have significant potential to improve these students' social and emotional health. Educator allies can also help to mitigate the differences that currently exist between transgender and cisgender students' academic outcomes.

In my experience, educators generally have a deep drive to support all students. We want them to learn, to grow as individuals and thinkers, and to feel safe and supported. Being an effective educator ally is often as simple as being open to learning from and listening to students—and it is the most important thing that we can do to foster environments where all students feel safe and able to learn.

Effective educator allies

- educate themselves on issues of gender diversity in order to feel knowledgeable enough to engage in dialogue;

- open the door to discussions of gender identity by using one's own pronoun when introducing themselves and leaving space for students to share their own gender, name, and pronoun;

- stand up to transphobia when they witness it from others;

- and most of all, listen to students and relate to each student on an individual level.

It's important to keep in mind that ALL students are different, so regardless of gender identity, there is no cookie-cutter approach that teachers can use to instantly meet every student's needs. However, there are some general approaches that are useful in creating a supportive environment for transgender and nonbinary students. It is my wish that regardless of your current level of understanding, by the end of this book, you will feel more empowered to create a safe and supportive space for everyone, including those with transgender and nonbinary identities.

When I work with schools to help them to create safe, inclusive, and equitable environments for all students, regardless of gender, I generally get asked the same question: "Why are you doing this?" It is because of student stories like the ones in this chapter. I come to this work both as an outsider and an insider; that is, as a cisgender female, I do not fit into the same gender identification cat-egory as the transgender or nonbinary students I write about. At the same time, as an arts administrator in the K–12 setting, teaching music and supervising visual and performing arts teachers, I am keenly aware of how these students are consistently underserved, ignored, and mistreated in school. We, as educators, must do better to meet the needs of these students in our schools.

It was this sense of purpose that shaped my doctoral research. Throughout the course of my studies, I worked with transgender and nonbinary students to learn directly from them about their educational experiences. Over the span of several months, they documented their experiences in words, photographs, and drawings. They have given me permission to share their stories with you, using pseudonyms. Their words underscore the reality that students who do not fit into cisgender norms face in schools today.

Meet the Students

Frankie is a whirling dervish of energy who literally tumbles through the door in the school counselor's office, where we have our first meeting. A student at a small public high school, he identifies as "a guy, just a dude." Art and theater are important parts of Frankie's identity, and he has been accepted to a noted performing arts college. His hands are stained with paint, and he wears a T-shirt for his current show, in which he has a lead part. He invites me to attend in the first five minutes of our meeting. Frankie describes himself as having ADD, and while he does get distracted throughout our conversations, he is extremely thoughtful and well-spoken. Frankie figured out he was queer ("That's a word I use. I know some people don't, but I use it") in eighth grade, but wasn't sure exactly what that meant for him. He describes himself as gay, and he's currently dating a cisgender gay boy at his school.

James, a college freshman, appears at first glance to be a typical high-achieving, socially active undergraduate. He is an officer in his fraternity, dating a pretty girl, and majoring in pre-law. When prompted, he suggests that if a person were to play him in a movie, it would be heartthrob Ryan Reynolds. One would never guess by looking at the confident, outgoing person he is now that during his K–12 experience, his mental health suffered immensely as a result of transphobic bullying by peers and teachers as he transitioned socially and medically.

Lavender identifies as female, nonbinary, or gender fluid. When prompted to provide a pronoun, Lavender suggests *he*, *she*, or *they*, finally pronouncing, "I don't care." They are quiet and shy, often smoothing back their dyed bright-blue hair as we converse. Lavender has experienced significant issues with depression since middle school, and feels isolated in high school. Lavender has not formally come out as trans, as categories are not an important part of their gender identity, but they are beginning to adopt more traditionally female styles of clothing. They describe fashion as a central part of their gender expression.

Robert is a quiet college freshman who meets me in a coffee shop on campus. A music composition major, he explains that he is currently directing a performance that will debut shortly. He leans forward as he speaks, looking at me seriously through his glasses. He describes himself as an "oddball" in school, especially after he cut his hair short in elementary school. His internal struggle increased in middle school, when people's bodies started developing and his own began to show "more characteristics of . . . the original gender." During this time, Robert was unaware of identities that were not cisgender: "I hadn't really heard the term [transgender]—I had heard the word before but didn't really know what it meant, it hadn't really been brought up anywhere, and so I figured, I'm just quirky, I'm just, you know, different." Robert experienced a significant amount of stress and frustration in school that compounded his academic struggles; he attributes this to the confusion of other students and school faculty regarding his gender: "I think a lot of people just didn't know, like, how to talk to me? They didn't know . . . should I talk to you like I talk to other guys, should I talk to you like—you know, they really didn't know, so that made it hard to connect with a lot of people."

Swan, although tiny, projects a powerful image and voice. They identify as gender queer, gender fluid, or nonbinary. Their gender expression varies dramatically over the course of our interactions: for our first meeting, Swan arrives in a hat, an over-sized flannel shirt, baggy jeans, hiking boots, and no makeup. The next time we speak, Swan wears a tight black dress, fishnet stockings, a bold cat's eye, and green lipstick. For Swan, fluidity in their gender expression is an important part of their identity. Considering this, attending an all-girls Catholic school where everyone is required to wear a uniform and LGBTQ identities are not acknowl-edged is challenging for Swan. They also lack support at home, as their family has rejected the idea that they are not female. Regardless of their personal struggles, Swan projects positivity and is doing well in school. They attribute their success to a strong friend group that is like a family.

Key Terms

The following is a VERY short list of additional terms related to this topic. There are many other excellent resources available (see the list at the end of this book for some ideas) that expand upon these terms and illuminate other words and phrases related to what is presented in the book. I encourage you to check them out!

Ally:

An individual committed to creating a safer and more equitable world for people who do not necessarily reflect their own racial, religious, cultural, gender, sexual (or other) identity.

Assigned Sex at Birth/Sex Assigned at Birth:

The sex included on one's original birth certificate.

Cisgender, Cis:

A Latin term, *cis* means *same*. Cisgender people have gender identities that align with their assigned gender at birth.

Dead Name:

The name on one's birth certificate that is no longer used.

Gender Expression:

Expression = External

This is how a person shows how they feel about their gender identity through clothing, hairstyles, mannerisms, and more.

" I describe [being gender fluid] usually as a chameleon effect—depending on what I feel as I wake up in the morning is how I try to present myself, at least in terms of gender expression … If I'm like, "Oh, I'm feeling really pretty today, I'm gonna wear a skirt," I'll do so. But if I wake up and I'm like, "Hmm, I don't think I'm feeling that feminine today," then maybe I'll do a combination of, like, a cute shirt but then maybe some sweatpants, or something that looks a little more neutral. And then if I'm feeling more masculine, then maybe I'll wear a flannel or something that tells everyone how I'm feeling. "

Gender Fluidity:

Cisgender, trans, and nonbinary people can all express gender fluidity in clothing, manner, etc. and still have a static gender identity. Other people may not always identify as always male or female, and their gender identity may vary through their lives, or even over the course of a day.

Gender Identity:

Identity = Internal

This is how a person feels inside in regard to their gender. Sometimes a person's gender identity aligns with their assigned biological sex at birth (the term for this is *cisgender*), and other times it does not. There are many terms for different gender identities, but in general, a person may identify as male, female, both, or neither.

Intersectionality:

How different components of a person's identity, including gender, sexuality, race, culture, religion, ability, and more overlap to contribute to how they see the world and how others view them. Issues of intersectionality also have the potential to increase discrimination against individuals and groups.

Microaggressions:

Intentional or unintentional insults or assumptions rooted in gender, race, or sexuality bias that a person encounters on a regular, daily basis.

Misgendering:

When an individual is referred to with incorrect gender identifiers/pronouns.

Nonbinary, Enby, N. B.:

These terms fall under the transgender umbrella and refer to individuals who are not cisgender and whose gender identities do not fall within a binary spectrum. *Gender nonconforming/GNC* or *gender queer* are other terms used to express this identity.

Sexuality:

Just as a cisgender person may be straight, gay, bisexual, asexual, etc., a transgender or nonbinary person's sexuality can also fall anywhere on the spectrum. Who a person is attracted to romantically or sexually is NOT dependent on their gender identity.

Transgender, Trans:

An umbrella term referring to individuals whose gender identity does not align with their assigned gender at birth. Note: the term is *transgender*, not *transgendered!*

Issue

Some educators are uncomfortable with discussing the issue of gender identity with students. However, avoiding the topic of gender only serves to reinforce the gender binary in schools, which ignores one of the most important elements of transgender and nonbinary students' identities.

It's OK to Acknowledge Transgender & Nonbinary Gender Identities

Educators can affirm that transgender and nonbinary students are welcome—AND help to set positive norms in schools at the same time—by acknowledging transgender and nonbinary identities.

First, using one's own pronouns in introductions is especially effective for two reasons: first, it sends a message that you are aware of and at least somewhat knowledgeable about issues of gender diversity. This practice also helps to normalize the practice of sharing pronouns, and emphasizes that we should not assume a person's pronouns based on appearance.

Some educators like to give their students a survey at the beginning of the year or semester to discover their interests, learning preferences, etc. Including an *optional* field for students to share the name and pronoun they would like for you to use in class may yield helpful and surprising results.

Keep in mind that some considerations must be made if including this field on a survey. First, make sure the information is kept confidential. If you have questions about what the student wrote, find a discreet way to check in with them. Also, when they're sitting among their peers, some students may not feel that they have enough privacy to answer this question. To this end, it's a good idea to avoid including this question at the beginning of a survey, when the class is most likely answering the same question at the same time.

"

I think there was so little knowledge and it was such a taboo thing to talk about that nobody wanted to say the wrong thing, and so they just decided that saying nothing and just pretending it wasn't there was best. I don't think they wanted to hurt me, I just think they didn't want to put their neck on the line, like it wasn't worth the risk for them to help one kid.

"

What You Can Do as an Ally:

- Share your pronouns:
  - ▶ Introduce yourself with your own name and pronouns.
  - ▶ Include your pronouns in your email signature.
- Display gender-inclusive signs in your classroom. (Free stickers and posters are available at www.glsen.org.)

- Avoid the term *preferred pronoun* and instead ask, "What is the pronoun I should use when referring to you in class?"
- Be aware that some students may feel most comfortable not being referred to with a pronoun at all. They may prefer to be referred to by name only. Although this may feel repetitive, do honor this request.

Issue

Sex-separated facilities such as bathrooms and locker rooms are frequently unsafe environments for transgender and nonbinary students, who are often harassed when using sex-specific spaces. As a result, approximately two-thirds of transgender and nonbinary students avoid using these spaces whenever possible while at school out of fear or discomfort.

Many transgender and nonbinary students use the bathroom in the school's nursing office. However, the nurse's office is often far from their classes and, on larger campuses, may be in a completely different building. If students are required to change clothes before and after PE, transgender and nonbinary students might opt to wait for other students to leave the locker room, which can mean arriving to their next class late.

"Since I was four years old I'd get weird looks when I'd go into the women's room … in school I had to use the bathroom in the nurse's office. They were pretty respectful there."

———————————

"We actually have a gender-neutral bathroom here, but I don't use it at all. For whatever reason, I would rather use the women's bathroom than use the gender-neutral one just because it makes me feel different."

It's OK to Consider the Physical Needs of Transgender & Nonbinary Students

All students should be allowed the option of using the bathroom and locker rooms that align with their gender identity. Many schools offer gender-neutral bathrooms that are open to all students, regardless of gender. (Some schools have even had success removing gender-based restrooms altogether and offering only gender-neutral bathrooms.)

Unfortunately, even in schools that offer a gender-neutral bathroom, transgender and nonbinary students may be targeted or feel uncomfortable using it. For this reason, transgender and nonbinary students should have options regarding where to use the restroom.

What You Can Do as an Ally:

- Provide students with adequate time to access the restroom of their choice. Keep in mind that they may be most comfortable using a nurse's office, which may be in a different part of campus.

- Advocate for "All Gender" bathrooms in your school and communicate to all students and faculty that these are available to anyone who wants to use them.

- If a student consistently comes to class late, take a moment to look at their schedule. Do they have PE immediately before your class?

- If a cisgender student expresses discomfort at sharing facilities with a transgender student, offer another option, such as using a bathroom in a nurse's office, for the student who is uncomfortable. The transgender student's access to the bathroom should not hinge on others' comfort level about sharing the bathroom.

Issue

Dress code policies often include unnecessary gendered language and assume that all students choose to wear clothing traditionally associated with a binary gender. But many students, transgender and cisgender alike, like to flaunt fashion "rules" and play with gender in their fashion choices. In the interest of equity, dress codes should extend to students of all genders.

It's OK to Revamp That Dress Code!

Students often use clothing as part of their gender expression. Considering that fashion can be such an integral component of gender expression, educators and schools have a responsibility to assess how dress codes are communicated, to be conscious of how a transgender or nonbinary student may feel when reading these types of policies, and to adopt more gender-neutral language.

Gendered Language	Other Options to Try
Girls should not wear spaghetti straps.	Students should not wear spaghetti straps.
Boys must wear black pants, girls must wear black pants or long black skirts.	Performers must wear black pants or long black skirts.

These types of simple changes can be made at no cost to schools. In my own practice as a district administrator, I have advocated for changes like these, and often the response from other administrators has been, "We can do that—but what's the big deal?" However, for many students, this IS a big deal. While cisgender people might not perceive gendered language to be an issue, for transgender and nonbinary students, gender-neutral language promotes a sense of inclusion rather than exclusion.

"

Definitely there's times where I get more confidence from clothing now. Sometimes I feel like people are like staring or whatever if I'm in a very girly outfit or something. But in general people are cool, and if they don't have anything nice to say, they don't say anything to my face, which I appreciate.

"

Issue

Often, educators use gendered language and practices without even realizing it. This can be confusing, embarrassing, or frightening for students who may not fit into what some educators perceive to be traditional gender roles and who experience these types of microaggressions many times throughout the course of each day.

It's OK to Avoid Gendered Language & Practices

In most cases, educators use gendered language because it's what they are used to, or what they've done in the past. Simply becoming aware of using gendered language is the first step in rectifying its overuse in classrooms.

Are there times when you use gendered language in your classroom? If so, why? What types of adjustments can you make to the phrasing you use to alleviate some of the stress it may cause transgender and nonbinary students?

Gendered Language/Practice	Other Options to Try
"Boys and girls" "Ladies and gentlemen"	Class/Everyone/People/Students/Learners/Artists/Musicians/Writers/Scientists/Investigators/Y'all … etc.
Grouping students by gender to line up, collect materials, or engage in an activity	Separate students by clothing color, favorite season, etc.
"Please remind your son/daughter …"	"Please remind your child …"
Assigning lockers, cubbies, or seats by gender	Mix it up! Assign by alphabetical order or experiment with how different groupings help with classroom management.

"I remember being very confused when people would separate things by gender. They would say, "Boys on one side and girls on the other," and I would freeze and everyone would laugh because they thought I was kidding, but I was genuinely confused as to where I was supposed to go because the person that I viewed myself as and the person that everybody else viewed me as was so different."

Issue

There is a lot of language involved in discussing gender identities. This can be frustrating for some educators, who may pull back from engaging in discussions because they feel like they may say the wrong thing. The following is a quote from a recent educator training session that I facilitated. Does this sound familiar to you?

I feel like I'm really behind or I missed the discussion, because I'm really weak on understanding the terms. You know, I think in our school we started with LGBQ and now there's nonbinary, transgender . . . then I know there's the question of pronouns, and I get really totally tongue-tied because I don't know. Is it when someone is nonbinary when the pronoun issue comes, or is it when someone is a lesbian when the pronoun issue comes? I don't have the knowledge I need to really approach it in a sensitive way.

This educator genuinely cares for her students and is invested in fostering an inclusive environment, but is nervous about causing further harm to them. As a result, she avoids engaging in using vocabulary related to gender identities.

It's OK to Mirror Language

Each individual uses different vocabulary to describe gender-related phenomena, and students themselves may not use the "proper terminology" when describing their own experience. For example, when discussing their dead names (the assigned name at birth that is no longer used), students may use various terms, including *legal name*, *given name*, *birth name*, or *dead name*.

The good news for educators is, it's not about knowing all the "right" vocabulary. One of the most important things educators can do to support their students, including transgender and nonbinary students, is to listen to the language students use themselves and then adopt that language. By listening to students' own descriptions of what they are experiencing, educators can support them by using the students' own lexicon.

Issue

Transgender and nonbinary youths who use pronouns other than those aligned with their assigned sex at birth are often addressed with the wrong pronouns. This is uncomfortable and potentially emotionally triggering. This problem is somewhat specific to the English language, though certainly not exclusive to it. While many languages use a gender-neutral third-person pronoun or do not use gender pronouns at all, old-school English uses gendered pronouns such as *he* and *him*, and *she* and *hers*—and some educators are reluctant to accept evolution of language in relation to gender.

It's OK to Accept That Language Evolves

Ungendered pronouns (also referred to as gender-neutral or neo-gender pronouns) have existed in English at least since the late 1800s. Today, there are more choices for those who do not wish to use gendered pronouns. Besides *they*, some other examples of nonbinary pronouns include *zie/hir/hirs/hirself* or *xie/xyr/xyrs/xyrself*.

This is really the tip of the iceberg, but educators, take a deep breath! We are already so adept at adjusting our teaching practices as we learn what's most effective and how to best support students' social-emotional well-being. As educators, we have the skill set and can make the effort to differentiate for students who use nonbinary pronouns.

Issue

Some educators resist using *they* as a pronoun for an individual student because doing so conflicts with grammatical rules enforced during the teacher's own educational experiences. Again, refusing to use a student's pronoun based on personal bias is not only unproductive in learning environments, but also damaging to students who use this pronoun.

It's OK to Use *They* as a Singular Pronoun

They **is perfectly acceptable** as a singular pronoun, and it has been for centuries. Etymologists estimate that as far back as the 1300s *they* has been used as a gender-neutral pronoun. Current APA and *Chicago Manual of Style* writing guidelines suggest that the singular use of *they* is acceptable when referring to an individual who uses this pronoun.

Saying *they* as a singular pronoun may take getting used to if you have not done it before, but keep in mind that using the correct pronoun is integral to making students with this pronoun feel like they belong, and Merriam-Webster recently updated the singular definition of *they* to specifically refer to a nonbinary pronoun used by some people.

How Is *They* Singular Used in Different Cases?

Subject   Sam did a much better job following the rules in class today.
They received a sticker for doing so well.

Object   "If you love somebody, set **them** free."

—Sting

Possessive   "There's not a man I meet but doth salute me
As if I were **their** well-acquainted friend."

—Shakespeare, from *A Comedy of Errors*, act 4, scene 3

Reflexive   "Now leaden slumber with life's strength doth fight;
And every one to rest **themselves** betake,
Save thieves, and cares, and troubled minds, that wake."

—Shakespeare, from *The Rape of Lucrece*, stanza 18

Hold on . . .

What about an honorific (Ms./Mr./Mrs./Miss) for people who use they/them/theirs pronouns?

Just use Mx. (pronounced "Mix")!

What You Can Do as an Ally

■ Consistently use correct pronouns (the pronouns they request) for all students.

■ Practice, practice, practice! If a student changes their pronoun from one you are used to, visualize the student and practice using the correct pronoun.

■ Always refer to a student with their current pronoun, even when talking about the past when the pronoun may have been different.

■ If you are just learning to use *they* as a singular pronoun and find yourself tripping over the word, try using it to describe your pet over the course of a day: "Mitzy ate all of their food today! What a good dog." This practice can help to get you comfortable with use of the singular *they* (and the dog won't care!).

Issue

Transgender and nonbinary students who use a name other than their assigned name at birth are often accidentally or intentionally addressed by their dead names by teachers, substitutes, administrators, and secretaries, or on rosters. This can cause significant anxiety and discomfort for these youths.

It's OK to Call Students by the Names They Choose

Consistently using a transgender student's name correctly sends a signal to them that they are cared for and validated. It also models for other educators and students what's acceptable and appropriate. Using correct student names is not only important for individual teachers, but is also integral for schools themselves. Schools must make accommodations to ensure that students' dead names are not included in materials whenever possible.

Some schools have addressed this issue by working with the electronic data provider to include the student's chosen name on all internal documents, such as rosters, while keeping the student's assigned name at birth on state reporting data and grading information that is accessible by parents. Other schools have accepted a letter from a student's parents giving permission to change all documents or have even allowed a student to reenroll with a different name after submitting an updated passport with the new name.

Approaching this issue thoughtfully—and discussing preferences with each student—will help to alleviate the trauma students experience as a result of educator missteps or bureaucratic miscommunications and mistakes.

"Substitutes. That's the worst. It's such a stressful thing when they're calling attendance and you're waiting and you have to raise your hand. Um, that's just, like, the worst."

"I had a teacher—he made a comment that I will NEVER forget. He called me by my birth name as a punishment in front of my entire class. "

" My legal name showed up on the voting list for prom queens because they just copied and pasted. And they did apologize, but I was upset. "

What You Can Do as an Ally

- If a student asks to be called a different name, honor their request. After all, we're used to using students' chosen names or nicknames for a variety of reasons in our classes.

- If you'll be out, plan ahead to leave updated rosters for substitutes so that in your absence your students are referred to by the names they request.

- Consider who's aware of the student's gender identity. Be careful to avoid outing a student if they have shared personal information with you they have not shared with others.

Issue

Transgender and nonbinary students rarely see their gender identities represented in literature or curricula in schools.

You may be familiar with the work of Dr. Rudine Sims Bishop, professor emerita at Ohio State University, who focuses on the importance of racial diversity in children's literature, not only so students can see themselves reflected in literature, but also so others can gain insight regarding people with different backgrounds. She writes:

Books are sometimes windows, offering views of worlds that may be real or imagined, familiar or strange. These windows are also sliding glass doors, and readers have only to walk through in imagination to become part of whatever world has been created and recreated by the author. When lighting conditions are just right, however, a window can also be a mirror. Literature transforms human experience and reflects it back to us, and in that reflection we can see our own lives and experiences as part of the larger human experience. Reading, then, becomes a means of self-affirmation, and readers often seek their mirrors in books.

It's OK to Represent Transgender & Nonbinary Identities in Curriculum

Just as it is integral for students to read and learn about those with diverse racial identities, it is extremely valuable for students to see transgender and nonbinary identities represented in literature and curricula in schools.

What You Can Do as an Ally

- Assess whether the literature selection for classes and in libraries includes texts with transgender and nonbinary characters. If the literature is not inclusive, initiate a conversation with those who make selections about books in the district to see if these texts may be made available for students.

- In your own teaching, include transgender and nonbinary individuals in lists/visual displays of famous scientists, composers, film directors, etc.

- Determine whether your school's health education curriculum acknowledges transgender and nonbinary identities. If it does not, what steps can be made to adjust the curriculum to be more inclusive?

Issue

The fear of making mistakes and causing trauma for students can be paralyzing for some well-intentioned educators. The following is a quote from a teacher I recently spoke with about her approaches to supporting transgender students. Does the following statement sound familiar to you?

*I've had some transgender kids, and I've tried very hard to support them, but I probably went overboard trying not to say the **wrong** thing—that's definitely an issue that I have. It is a situation where I get very concerned about possibly doing something wrong and years later that person might still be thinking about it.*

Sometimes, if a teacher does accidentally misgender a student, they feel so guilty that they exhibit a strong emotional response that then requires the student (the one who was just misgendered) to comfort the teacher.

It's OK to Make a Mistake

Everybody makes mistakes. If you make an honest mistake, for example using *she* for a student who uses *they*, simply correct yourself and move on. A long speech about how sorry you are will only make the student feel uncomfortable.

Don't forget that being open to feedback from students is an important part of being an educator ally. If a student suggests that you try new terminology, listen to them without being defensive. You may learn something important—and forge deeper connections with the student.

Issue

Gender identity and expression may change over time, and the gender journey can take many forms. Some people adopt transgender or nonbinary labels at some point after exhibiting gender nonconforming characteristics and behavior. Cisgender youth may also express gender nonconforming traits. For educators who have not experienced these phenomena, it may be challenging to understand at first.

It's OK to Support Students Where They Are Now

An educator's role is to foster environments wherein all students feel safe and supported so that they can learn. Part of this is understanding that gender identity is a phenomenon that may evolve throughout a child's development. It is our responsibility as educators to make it clear that no matter what, we will accept and respect the identity and expression of all of our students, regardless of where they may be on their personal journeys.

The process of understanding and coming to terms with one's own gender identity can be complex and difficult to acknowledge and share with others. Some may never feel comfortable sharing this information publicly. Some may reveal information about their gender identity in layers. It's crucial to remember that simply by expressing behavior, dress, or other characteristics that do not align with the sex assigned at birth, students can be at increased risk for bullying, marginalization, and violence—this is true whether students are transgender or cisgender.

What You Can Do as an Ally

- Keep the door open for conversations about gender identity, but never force it.

- Reintroduce yourself with pronouns at the beginning of each year or term in order to acknowledge possible pronoun and name changes in others that may evolve over time.

"

In high school I started doing a lot of research, and I wrote a lot of research papers about transgender and the gay community, and I kind of found out, "Oh—this is where I belong!"

"

———————————

"

I was like, "Am I lesbian?" And then turns out I wasn't. One day, I was, like, walking to my next class, and I was wearing this shirt that I just couldn't stand anymore—when I put it on that morning I thought I looked good, but I looked good as a girl. And I wasn't a girl. And I was walking to class and I could just feel it on me, and I looked around and there's all these other kids walking around just super comfortable with themselves, and they are not having that issue, and I just couldn't deal with it anymore.

"

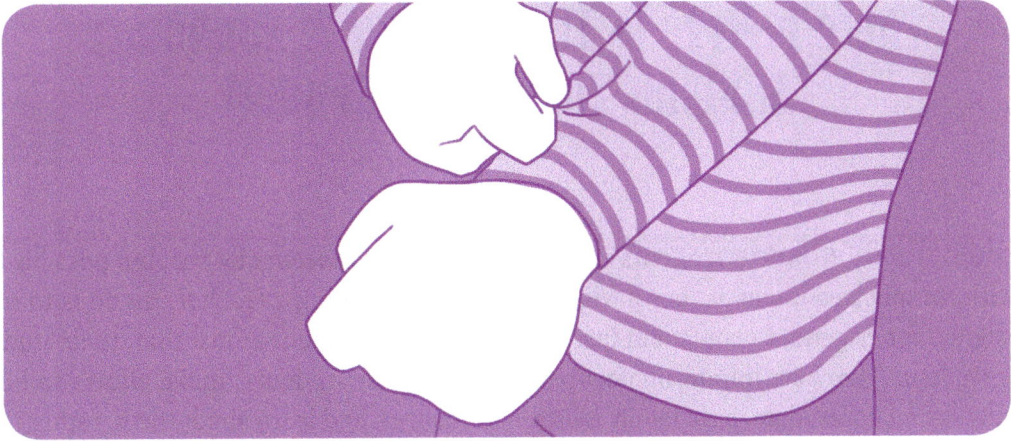

Finally, It's OK to Understand That There Is More to Transgender & Nonbinary Students Than Their Gender!

Transgender and nonbinary students may be dealing with complicated issues as they navigate a world designed for cisgender people, but just like cisgender students, they have important peer relationships, make mistakes, date, have family issues, and engage in sports, theater, music, or hobbies.

This may seem obvious, but possibly the most important thing a teacher can do is to treat each individual student as just that: their student. Listen to your students, make efforts to build relationships, and learn about them, rather than making assumptions.

" I always felt like I was having to tell teachers it was okay to treat me like everybody else, and it seemed like they were timid around me or like they had to be so, like, gentle with me?

I liked teachers who just treated me like everybody else, like just a normal kid, it's like a part of who you are but not, like, a debilitating character flaw. "

"

I can't speak for everyone, but I just wanted to be treated like a regular kid because I am a regular kid, but a lot of people don't see me as a regular kid. I think the most disheartening thing is being in a class and being treated like you're different. Everyone's got obstacles they have to face. It's just that ours are a little easier to see. We're all dealing with stuff, it's just that ours is easier to see. All I need is to be treated and thought of as what I am just like, you know, a dude in high school, just a high school boy.

"

It's OK to Plan Ahead!

Now that you have read the book, take a moment to consider the following situations. What steps could you take to be an effective ally to transgender and nonbinary students in each of these circumstances?

- You notice that your colleague in elementary school lines students up by gender to go to recess.

- Sam, a kindergartener who was assigned male at birth, has begun wearing dresses to school. Sam's parents let you know that they support Sam's clothing choices, but are worried Sam might be asked questions about wearing traditionally feminine clothing by the other students in class.

- Your high school's health curriculum does not include any information about gender diversity.

- Your colleague expresses frustration at a school counselor's request to use *they/them/theirs* pronouns for a student who previously used *she/her/hers* pronouns.

- Your school has no gender-neutral bathrooms.

- You use a *he* pronoun by mistake for a student who has begun to use *she*.

- A student visits you because he does not want to share a bathroom with a transgender student.

Extra Credit Exercises

- Practice introducing yourself with your pronouns out loud ("Hi, I'm Mr. Williams. My pronouns are he/him/his").

- See how long you can go throughout your regular day without using gendered pronouns.

- Read an excerpt from a novel to yourself and replace all gendered pronouns with singular *they/them/their* or *zie/hir/hirs/hirself* pronouns as practice.

It's OK to Learn More! Recommended Resources for Educator Allies

Resource	Description
Airton, Lee. *Gender: Your Guide: A Gender-Friendly Primer on What to Know, What to Say, and What to Do in the New Gender Culture*. Avon: Adams Media, 2019.	Wide-ranging, well-organized, and enjoyable read by a leader in the field of gender and sexual diversity in K–12 and teacher education.
Airton, Lee. They Is My Pronoun. Accessed 2019. http://www.theyismypronoun.com/.	Visit this site! Besides providing so much helpful information for cis and trans people alike—including crisis resources—the site also offers a link to ask anonymous questions.
Bongiovanni, Archie, and Tristan Jimerson. *A Quick & Easy Guide to They/Them Pronouns*. Portland: Limerence Press, 2018.	Fun, illustrated guide that delves deeply into they/them pronoun use.
Brill, Stephanie and Rachel Pepper. *The Transgender Child: A Handbook for Families and Professionals*. San Francisco: Cleis Press, 2008.	Helpful guidebook for parents, mental health caregivers, and educators.
Collins, Cory, and Jey Ehrenhalt. "Best Practices for Serving LGBTQ Students." 2018. *https://www.tolerance.org/magazine/publications/best-practices-for-serving-lgbtq-students*.	Districts can use this! Highlights: list of inclusive curriculum resources, glossary of terms, and school checklist addressing how well a school meets the needs of students.

Gender Spectrum. "Using Gender Inclusive Language with Students." 2017. https://www.genderspectrum.org/resources/education-2/.

User-friendly instruction on how to use gender-inclusive language in the K–12 classroom.

Mady G., and J. R. Zuckerberg. *A Quick & Easy Guide to Queer & Trans Identities.* Portland: Limerence Press, 2019.

Entertaining, illustrated guide to the basics of the LGBT+ world.

National Center for Transgender Equality. "School Action Center." 2019. https://transequality.org/school-action-center.

Comprehensive site offering information about legal rights, state guidelines, tips for schools, support groups, and many other resources.

Orr, Asaf, Joel Baum, Jay Brown, Elizabeth Gill, Ellen Kahn, and Anna Salem. "Schools in Transition: A Guide to Supporting Transgender Students in K–12 Schools." Genderspectrum.org. 2015. https://www.genderspectrum.org/staging/wp-content/uploads/2015/08/Schools-in-Transition-2015.pdf.

A guide sponsored by the ACLU, Gender Spectrum, Human Rights Campaign (HRC), National Center for Lesbian Rights, and National Education Association that addresses issues including student records, legal considerations, facilities, and gender support and transition plans for K–12 schools.

Shlasko, Davey. *Trans Allyship Workbook: Building Skills to Support Trans People in Our Lives.* Think Again Training, 2017. http://thinkagaintraining.com/resources/publications/trans-ally-workbook/.

Amazing guide for trans inclusion! Includes guidelines for thinking and asking about pronouns, a list of possible pronouns and how they are used, and much more.

Gender Reveal Podcast. https://gender.libsyn.com/.

Highly entertaining and edifying podcast by journalist Molly Woodstock that centers on nonbinary and transgender folks. Available on Spotify, iHeartRadio, and basically anywhere you listen to podcasts.

References

Airton, Lee. *Gender: Your Guide: A Gender-Friendly Primer on What to Know, What to Say, and What to Do in the New Gender Culture.* Avon: Adams Media, 2019.

American Psychological Association. *Publication Manual of the American Psychological Association,* 6th ed. Washington, DC: American Psychological Association, 2010.

Baron, Dennis E. "The Epicene Pronoun: The Word That Failed." *American Speech* 56, no. 2 (1981): 83–97.

Dessel, Adrienne, Alex Kulick, Laura Wernick, and Daniel Sullivan. "The Importance of Teacher Support: Differential Impacts by Gender and Sexuality." *Journal of Adolescence* 56 (2017): 136–44.

Dictionary.com. "It's Okay to Use 'They' to Describe One Person: Here's Why." 2018. https://www.dictionary.com/e/they-is-a-singular-pronoun/.

Gattis, Maurice, and Sara McKinnon. *School Experiences of Transgender and Gender Non-Conforming Students in Wisconsin.* Madison: GSAFE, 2015.

Jones, Steve. *CyberSociety: Computer-Mediated Communication and Community.* Thousand Oaks: Sage Publications, 1995.

Kosciw, Joseph, Emily Greytak, Adrian Zongrone, Caitlin Clark, and Nhan Truong. *The 2017 National School Climate Survey: The Experiences of Lesbian, Gay, Bisexual and Transgender Youth in Our Nation's Schools.* New York: GLSEN, 2017.

Lynn M. O'Connell, Jana G. Atlas, Anita L. Saunders, and Rebecca Philbrick. "Perceptions of Rural School Staff Regarding Sexual Minority Students." *Journal of LGBT Youth* 7, no. 4 (2010): 293–309.

Orr, Asaf, Joel Baum, Jay Brown, Elizabeth Gill, Ellen Kahn, and Anna Salem. "Schools in Transition: A Guide to Supporting Transgender Students in K–12 Schools." Genderspectrum.org. 2015. https://www.genderspectrum.org/staging/wp-content/uploads/2015/08/Schools-in-Transition-2015.pdf.

Shonkoff, Jack, and Susan Bales. "Science Does Not Speak for Itself: Translating Child Development Research for the Public and Its Policymakers." *Child Development* 82, no. 1 (2011): 17–32.

Sims Bishop, Rudine. "Mirrors, Windows, and Sliding Glass Doors." *Perspectives* 1, no. 3 (1990): ix–xi.

National Survey on LGBTQ Mental Health. *The Trevor Project.* New York: The Trevor Project, 2019.

The GenIUSS Group. "Best Practices for Asking Questions to Identify Transgender and Other Gender Minority Respondents on Population-Based Surveys." Edited by Jody L. Herman. Los Angeles: The Williams Institute, 2014.

Whittlesey, Christina. "Translations: Exploring and Sharing Experiences of Transgender and Non-Binary Students." Unpublished doctoral dissertation, 2019. https://search.proquest.com/openview/2723f3460 44d544ae070bf4c0142bc75/1?pq-origsite=gscholar &cbl=18750&diss=y.

Wozolek, Boni, Lindsey Wootton, and Aaron Demlow. "The School-to-Coffin Pipeline: Queer Youth, Suicide, and Living the In-Between." *Cultural Studies ↔ Critical Methodologies* 17, no. 5 (2017): 392–8.

About the Author

Christy Whittlesey, PhD (she/her/hers), is an educator and school administrator who has worked in settings ranging from PreK to higher education for almost twenty years.

Christy received her PhD specializing in research and evaluation in education from the University of Massachusetts Lowell in 2019, where her work exploring the educational experiences of transgender and nonbinary students garnered her the Education Department's Outstanding Dissertation Award.

Christy regularly collaborates with teachers, administrators, and schools to develop plans and support educators in supporting inclusivity, diversity, and equity in their districts. She has presented on this topic at many conferences, including the SouthCoast Education Summit on Social-Emotional Learning, the Massachusetts School Administrators' Association, the National Art Education Association Conference, the Eastern Sociological Society Conference, the International Congress of Qualitative Inquiry, and the New England Educational Research Organization, among others.

Christy lives in Massachusetts with her husband, fellow educator and author Roger Whittlesey III, and their dog Kaylee.

About the Illustrator

Mordecai Vezina (he/him/his) is an animation student at the Massachusetts College of Art and Design. As a trans person who recently graduated from high school, this topic is close to his heart.

Before attending college, Mordy participated in seven years of musical theater, and was highly involved in both the Massachusetts Education-al Theater Guild and the International Thespian Society. Now he seeks to bring what he's learned from performance art to his work in animation and illustration.

When he's not away at school, Mordy lives in Massachusetts with his family and three pets, Mina, Olive, and Harry.

More from Dave Burgess Consulting, Inc.

DAVE BURGESS Consulting, Inc.

Since 2012, DBCI has been publishing books that inspire and equip educators to be their best. For more information on our DBCI titles or to purchase bulk orders for your school, district, or book study, visit daveburgess.com/dbc-books.

More from the Like a PIRATE™ Series

Teach Like a PIRATE by Dave Burgess

eXPlore Like a Pirate by Michael Matera

Learn Like a Pirate by Paul Solarz

Play Like a Pirate by Quinn Rollins

Run Like a Pirate by Adam Welcome

Lead Like a PIRATE™ Series

Lead Like a PIRATE by Shelley Burgess and Beth Houf

Balance Like a Pirate by Jessica Cabeen, Jessica Johnson, and Sarah Johnson

Lead beyond Your Title by Nili Bartley

Lead with Culture by Jay Billy

Lead with Literacy by Mandy Ellis

Leadership & School Culture

Culturize by Jimmy Casas

Escaping the School Leader's Dunk Tank by Rebecca Coda and Rick Jetter

From Teacher to Leader by Starr Sackstein

The Innovator's Mindset by George Couros

Kids Deserve It! by Todd Nesloney and Adam Welcome

Let Them Speak by Rebecca Coda and Rick Jetter

The Limitless School by Abe Hege and Adam Dovico

The Pepper Effect by Sean Gaillard

The Principled Principal by Jeffrey Zoul and Anthony McConnell

Relentless by Hamish Brewer

The Secret Solution by Todd Whitaker, Sam Miller, and Ryan Donlan

Start. Right. Now. by Todd Whitaker, Jeffrey Zoul, and Jimmy Casas

Stop. Right. Now. by Jimmy Casas and Jeffrey Zoul

They Call Me "Mr. De" by Frank DeAngelis

Unmapped Potential by Julie Hasson and Missy Lennard

Word Shift by Joy Kirr

Your School Rocks by Ryan McLane and Eric Lowe

Technology & Tools

50 Things You Can Do with Google Classroom by Alice Keeler and Libbi Miller

50 Things to Go Further with Google Classroom by Alice Keeler and Libbi Miller

140 Twitter Tips for Educators by Brad Currie, Billy Krakower, and Scott Rocco

Block Breaker by Brian Aspinall

Code Breaker by Brian Aspinall

Google Apps for Littles by Christine Pinto and Alice Keeler

Master the Media by Julie Smith

Shake Up Learning by Kasey Bell

Social LEADia by Jennifer Casa-Todd

Teaching Math with Google Apps by Alice Keeler and Diana Herrington

Teachingland by Amanda Fox and Mary Ellen Weeks

Teaching Methods & Materials

All 4s and 5s by Andrew Sharos

The Classroom Chef by John Stevens and Matt Vaudrey

Ditch That Homework by Matt Miller and Alice Keeler

Ditch That Textbook by Matt Miller

Don't Ditch That Tech by Matt Miller, Nate Ridgway, and Angelia Ridgway

EDrenaline Rush by John Meehan

Educated by Design by Michael Cohen, The Tech Rabbi

The EduProtocol Field Guide by Marlena Hebern and Jon Corippo

The EduProtocol Field Guide: Book 2 by Marlena Hebern and Jon Corippo

Instant Relevance by Denis Sheeran

LAUNCH by John Spencer and A.J. Juliani

Make Learning MAGICAL by Tisha Richmond

Pure Genius by Don Wettrick

The Revolution by Darren Ellwein and Derek McCoy

Shift This! by Joy Kirr

Spark Learning by Ramsey Musallam

Sparks in the Dark by Travis Crowder and Todd Nesloney

Table Talk Math by John Stevens

The Wild Card by Hope and Wade King

The Writing on the Classroom Wall by Steve Wyborney

Inspiration, Professional Growth & Personal Development

Be REAL by Tara Martin

Be the One for Kids by Ryan Sheehy

Creatively Productive by Lisa Johnson

The EduNinja Mindset by Jennifer Burdis

Empower Our Girls by Lynmara Colón and Adam Welcome

The Four O'Clock Faculty by Rich Czyz

How Much Water Do We Have? by Pete and Kris Nunweiler

P Is for Pirate by Dave and Shelley Burgess

A Passion for Kindness by Tamara Letter

(Continued on next page)

Inspiration, Professional Growth & Personal Development (cont.)

The Path to Serendipity by Allyson Apsey

Sanctuaries by Dan Tricarico

Shattering the Perfect Teacher Myth by Aaron Hogan

Stories from Webb by Todd Nesloney

Talk to Me by Kim Bearden

Teach Me, Teacher by Jacob Chastain

TeamMakers by Laura Robb and Evan Robb

Through the Lens of Serendipity by Allyson Apsey

The Zen Teacher by Dan Tricarico

Children's Books

Beyond Us by Aaron Polansky

Cannonball In by Tara Martin

Dolphins in Trees by Aaron Polansky

I Want to Be a Lot by Ashley Savage

The Princes of Serendip by Allyson Apsey

Zom-Be a Design Thinker by Amanda Fox

www.ingramcontent.com/pod-product-compliance
Lightning Source LLC
Chambersburg PA
CBHW080405270326
41927CB00015B/3352